This 1995 edition published by
Derrydale Books,
distributed by
Random House Value Publishing, Inc.
40 Engelhard Avenue, Avenel,
New Jersey 07001.

Random House
New York · Toronto · London · Sydney · Auckland

A CIP catalog record for this book
is available from
the Library of Congress.

Printed in China

ISBN 0-517-12122-0

My Counting Book

CAROL THOMPSON

DERRYDALE BOOKS
NEW YORK · AVENEL

One heavy hippo

Two plump penguins

Three cuddly cats

Four tough teddy bears

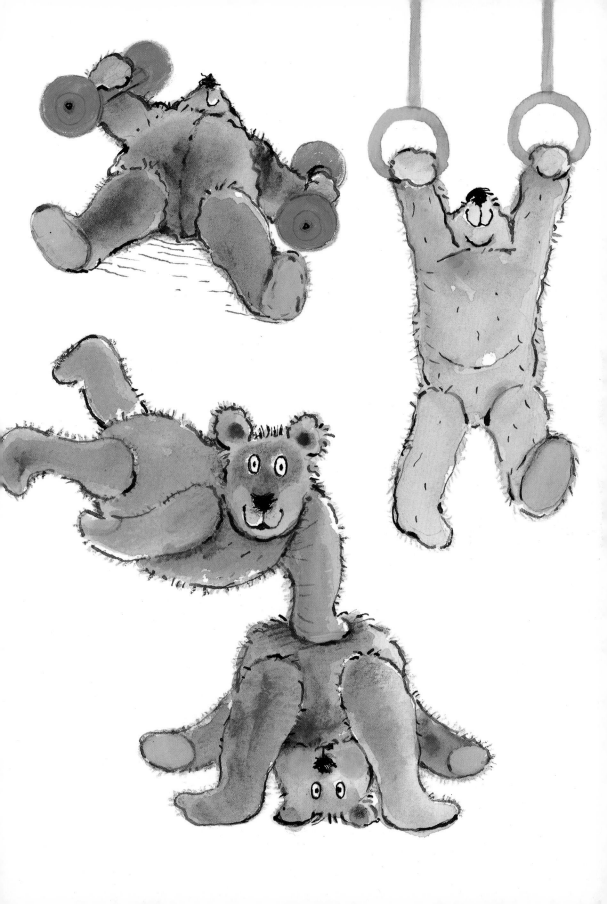

Five zebras crossing

Six swimming pigs

Seven leaping frogs

Eight fat hens

Nine nibbling rabbits

Ten peeping faces